Scenes in the Journey of Life

SCENES IN THE Journey OF LIFE

Joyce Amelia Marshall

XULON PRESS

Xulon Press
2301 Lucien Way #415
Maitland, FL 32751
407.339.4217
www.xulonpress.com

© 2023 by Joyce Amelia Marshall

All rights reserved solely by the author. The author guarantees all contents are original and do not infringe upon the legal rights of any other person or work. No part of this book may be reproduced in any form without the permission of the author.

Due to the changing nature of the Internet, if there are any web addresses, links, or URLs included in this manuscript, these may have been altered and may no longer be accessible. The views and opinions shared in this book belong solely to the author and do not necessarily reflect those of the publisher. The publisher therefore disclaims responsibility for the views or opinions expressed within the work.

Paperback ISBN-13: 978-1-66287-322-5
Ebook ISBN-13: 978-1-66287-323-2

Dedication

This book is dedicated, first, to my Lord and Savior, Jesus Christ, to whom I owe everything; then to my sisters: Brenda and Janette Marshall, and my brother: Kenneth Marshall, for giving me my inspiration to keep writing; and to my church family at Bethel AME Church in Boston, Massachusetts, for their support and encouragement in this endeavor. 10/19/22

Introduction

I accepted Jesus Christ as my Lord and Savior in 1976. I began writing poetry not long after that, as a way to process my thoughts and feelings, to sort through the changes happening in my life. I had my first few poems on sheets of loose-leaf paper. I shared them with one of my co-workers at the time, who encouraged me to keep writing, and gave me a hardcover book with blank pages and a blue construction paper book cover. Today, the blue has faded and there are rips in the paper, but this "blue book" is now the repository of my spiritual journey, my way of dissecting where I was from where I am now, scenes from my journey in life. There are still many blank pages left in that book; inspiring me to document my continued walk with the Lord. This tells me two things: that my story isn't over and there's space for me to grow in my Christian life. I hope this book encourages you to create your own scenes; to document your own journey; to use whatever gifts, skills and talents the Lord has given you to tell your story. All of our stories are important and valuable. All of us have a voice. All of us deserve to be heard. 10/19/22-11/29/22

About the author

Joyce Marshall was born and raised in Ava, New York. She moved to Massachusetts in 1973 and has lived in the state since then. She has been a registered nurse since 1982. 10/19/22-11/29/22

Forward

I have known the author for her entire life and have watched as she evolved from the seed to the flower, as God took hold and formulated His plan. The gifts He had planted emerged, one gem after another. Poems that were hidden, now have had light shown upon them, changes made, colors brightened; from unsure to more confident, from sad shadows to her new thoughts of the joy of the Lord within her. This book shows what can happen with the gift of reflection, thoughts and faith in God. Words come together and make a magnificent tapestry. I am not only a sister in Christ, I am her blood sister. I am proud in both cases.

Gratefully yours,

Brenda Marshall

November 2005

Scenes in the Journey of Life (poem selection)

If life is just the dreams we seek,
our feet on solid ground;
and peaceful, calm relationships
with laughter all around;

Then in my dreams of happiness
I somehow missed the boat;
and with all tears and sadness,
no love would stay afloat

A silent gnawing feeling
from deep inside did dwell,
and pulled itself from where it lived,
then once again it fell

But when life is, and then is gone,
it somehow seems a crime;
it separates the things you've done
and how you've spent your time

I would this life were ended,
but such are dues to pay,
one must not forfeit payments
until he's earned his stay

I cannot makes excuses
for the way my life was led;
but if life is just the dreams we seek,
I guess I'm way ahead

God changed my darkness into light,
my nighttime into day;
His patience there
He took great care
to show me a better way

God had special plans for me
and friends along the way;
who God has sent
and all were meant
to show me a better way

His leading, guiding, loving care,
joy in my heart to stay;
and all are mine
for He took the time
to show me a better way

Where do I fit in your vast plans?
What is my life to be?
How do I share the infinite love
that you have given me?

How do I thank you for your peace?
Why did I wait so long?
Can I remember my life before,
a life without a song?

Where do I go to spread your Word?
Is there a place for me?
Will I know to convey the truth
that you have made me see?

Praise the Lord
for mighty peaks
which tower high
beyond our reach
then fall to valleys
far below
with velvet grass
or gleaming snow

Praise the Lord
for His great love
which comes to us
from far above!
Our Holy Father,
His loving touch
our God
who loves us very much

Praise the Lord
for awesome power
from moving mountains
to growing flowers
<u>Who</u> died for us
yet without sin?
Praise God!
Let's give
our lives to Him!

Above the stars and galaxies,
within the lakes and streams;
entwined inside the hearts of those
whose plans and hopes and dreams;

Reflect the glory of Your Name,
who sing Your triumph song;
who have that peace, serenity,
for which we hope and long

And God loves us unfailingly,
His loving arms outstretched;
to conquer principalities
from this world to the next

I sit here now, with pen in hand,
to capture what I feel;
my mind goes where I had not planned,
to where my thoughts are real

To stand outside my hopes and dreams,
and watch them come and go;
although they changed from
what they seemed
to what I came to know

Yet deeper still the fears and doubts
crept out from far within;
some died and then were weeded out
but others fell again

And when they fell, I felt the pain,
yet hope I was to reap;
they landed on a different plane
not nearly quite as deep

For from the center of my heart
came light of bright array;
there was no place for fear to start
for God had blocked the way

How do I write a song to Thee?
For when I cried, You came to me,
and through your grace you set me free:
yet I'm without a song

How do I tell the world of Thee?
For though I'm weak you let me see,
Your power, grace and majesty
and yet I can't be strong

How do I change my life for Thee?
For herein lies the mystery;
You chose me for Your family,
and showed me I belong

Gods' power is all too real to me,
I know that Christ's His son;
but somehow it alluded me,
that God and Christ are one

Then someone came to me tonight
and from the heart she cried;
a fact of which I had lost sight:
she told me Jesus died

I always pray, "in Jesus name"
but does He live in me?
My heart said no, and I'm to blame:
He died to set me free

My hope is that it's not too late,
that there is time to see;
though it's true that Jesus died
He still can live in me

I prayed and prayed about my needs,
depressed and in despair;
my head was down, I noticed not
that Christ was standing there

I searched the scriptures willingly,
so burdened with my cares;
my ears were closed, I listened not
to all my answered prayers

When I looked up and saw Him there,
confessed my sins to Him;
He forgave me, then remembered not
that I had even sinned

I'll have to go back home again,
to find out where my dreams have been;
it's hard to picture them again,
    they seem so different now

I thought I'd lost them for awhile,
it was so difficult to smile;
and so I walked the lonely miles
    depressed, yet free somehow

The road had seemed so strange to me,
I met a man from Galilee;
who stopped to keep me company
    and wiped my dusty brow

He said He died for all my sin,
I cried and gave my life to Him;
the road no longer looked so dim,
the sun shone through the clouds

I'm glad to be back home again,
for now my dreams are long lost friends;
my doubts and fears were conquered then
    and God is with me now

The love of God amazes me,
for what good have I done?
And though I turned away from Him
He gave His only son

The love of God amazes me,
it shines so rich and pure;
it glows within the hearts of those
whose destiny is sure

The love of God amazes me,
it shows to me my need;
to learn to give my burdens up
so Christ can intercede

The love of God amazes me,
to love despite my sin;
what better way to show <u>my</u> love
but to give my life to Him

Memories of the things I've left behind,
shadowed by the fear I felt inside;
Christ told me of the hope He knew I'd find:
He told me I was blind
but then He opened up my eyes

Thinking back before I saw the day,
when I let Christ into my heart to stay;
He told me of the price I'd have to pay:
He knew what I would say
but still He opened up the way

It's hard to wonder where I would have been,
living with an emptiness within;
when satan tries to fight I know who'll win:
Christ washed away my sin
I'm going to live my life for Him

Inspired by Psalms 25:8-14
The Lord is good and upright,
He shows to us the way;
He leads the humble justly,
and teaches them His way
His paths are paved with love and truth
for all who trust in Him:
Oh my God, for Thy name's sake
please pardon all my sin

Is there a man who fears the Lord?
He'll show to him His choice
His soul will know prosperity,
his family will rejoice;
they'll have a land that God's prepared
especially for them:
He'll counsel those who reverence Him,
reveal His truths to them

I see myself from far away,
a picture not too clear;
my need to focus in on Christ
is hindered by my fear;

of what He's calling me to do:
I've kept my distance there;
although, I know what God commands
is righteous, just and fair

I see He has His arms outstretched
no matter where I've been
He's there to help me when I fall,
to stand me up again

He hears my sometimes muffled cries
of agony and pain;
and calmly reaches out to me
amidst the stress and strain

Teach me Lord to take your love,
a love so pure and true;
for only then will I have strength
to give it back to you

As we go on our thoughts will change,
our attitudes within;
and, if the Lord is in our lives,
a consciousness of sin

There comes a time in all our lives
when we will have to choose;
and have to risk the very things
we never want to lose

And there will be a time for us
when all is said and done;
then all our possibilities
are narrowed down to one

For God gives us the option
and all we need to know;
He doesn't make us follow Him,
if we don't want to go

It takes a lot of courage
to decide to go with Him;
and life is never easy
when the devil's out to win

But with the trials He gives us strength
to live from day to day;
for since He sent His son for us
we've no more debt to pay

Existence like it's owner
stands frail and insecure;
with myriad uncertainties,
uneasy and unsure

It's language filled with similies
that no one understands;
and even what it manages
falls short of its demands

Yet deep inside it's searching
as for a long lost friend
while wearied opportunities
are coming to an end

But time cannot remember
a solitary verse;
a poem left unfinished in
a world left none the worse

It plays the game it has to,
a lonely citizen;
to wander through the streets alone
until it's home again

Inspired by Psalm 100
Let all the earth shout to the Lord
with joy and gladness serve;
and give Him, through our songs Of praise,
the honor He deserves

We know that He alone is God
and made us by Himself;
we know that all belongs to Him:
our love, our lives, our wealth

Go through His gates with thankfulness,
and in His courts with praise;
give thanks to Him and bless His name
for all His loving ways

We know the Lord is always good,
His kindness never fails;
though time and people hurry on
His faithfulness prevails

Inspired by Psalm 63:1-5
O God, though art my God,
I will seek thee earnestly;
for in a dry and weary land
my being thirsts for thee

To see Thy gloried power
I have entered in Thy house;
because Thy love excels all life
I praise Thee with my mouth

O God, I lift my hands,
I will bless Thee all my days;
for Thou has satisfied my soul,
my lips will offer praise

The storming clouds
The lightning's flare
The gath'ring gloom
The moon's dull glare
A sense of sadness and despair
A fleeting sense that God is there

A sense of dread
A world of care
A lack of strength
Depression's fare
Emotions more than one can bear
A growing sense that God is there

A glimpse of hope
A love so rare
The Savior's touch
A soul's repair
The Lord's embrace beyond compare
The knowing sense that God is there

Inspired by 2 Chronicles 7:14
If my people,
called by my name,
would humble themselves and pray—
I'd hear from heaven,
forgive their sin
and be their hope and stay

If they would pray
and seek my face,
and turn from their wicked ways—
I'd heal their land,
draw near to them
and follow them all their days

America, democracy,
protected by our God
Our freedom scored on battlefields
where bloody feet have trod

American theology
oft substitutes our Lord
replaced Him with a sovereign
the people will afford

American complacency
forgets to honor God
the one who's kept us safe and free
on this united sod

American recovery
Lord help us trust in thee
and send revival in the land
home of the brave and free

A life is but a gift from God
a certain length of time
the chance to use the circumstance
to falter or to climb

To travel forward and progress
or fall behind the curve
to use the time to honor God
to love Him and to serve

The time is given freely
the amount of time unknown
and only time can then reveal
the crop from seed that's sown

And God decides who lives and dies
it's hard to understand
or even to accept His choice
or see His sovereign plan

All that's left to do is pray
and stay close to the Lord
and cling to all the boundless strength
provided in His word

Crazy days of summer
Hazy thoughts of slumber
People on vacation
Plans for recreation

Campfires throwing sparks
Packed amusement parks
Hammocks joining trees
Driving SUVs

Tea and juice in powder
Traffic on the hour
Daylight lasting longer
Flower scents are stronger

Steaks begin to sizzle
Monkey in the middle
Concerts in the park
Action after dark

Tourists crowd the cities
Parents on committees
Sitting in the shade
Baseball games are played

Lounge chairs to the shed
Books have all been read
Special time with friends
Oops! It's Fall again!

Inspired by Philippians 4:8
Finally brothers, whatever is true
and noble and right,
let these thoughts be in you

Always be mindful of that which is pure
and lovely, admired,
make your love for God sure

Whatever is excellent, worthy of praise,
keep your minds on these things
for the rest of your days

Inspired by Jeremiah 29: 11-13
The Lord says,
"I know all the plans I have made,
to prosper, protect you
with hope all your days

If you will but call me,
draw near me and pray
I promise I'll listen
and hear what you say"

"If you would just seek me...",
our dear Lord declares,
"...with all of your heart
I'll be found by you there"

Is there a time when the Lord is not with us:
a season, a day, a year?
Can we hide from His presence;
sequestered, alone
and think that the Lord is not near?

Is there ever a space where the Lord
cannot reach us:
too deep or too far or too wide?
Can we drift to a place where the Lord
cannot see us,
where He cannot come alongside?

Is there ever a moment when He does not love us:
our present, our future, our past?
No, in all of these things we are more than just
conquerors
through Christ who'll be there to the last

Inspired by Ephesians 4: 26-32
Let the sun not go down while you're angry
Let the new day not dawn with your wrath
Do not give the devil a foothold,
you must choose a different path

Let he who has stolen steal no longer,
but find useful works for his hands
Let him give what he can to the needy,
let the Lord dictate all of his plans

Let no unwholesome talk frame your speaking
so it edifies all those who hear
Don't bring grief to the Spirit who sealed you
for the day of redemption that's near

Let all bitterness, slander, malice
and all rage and anger subdue
Be compassionate, kind and forgiving
since through Christ, God's forgiven you

A Psalm of Praise

I give you praise, Lord
I give you praise
For you are glorious
I give you praise
You're beyond what I can see,
yet you're deep inside of me
I give you praise, Lord
I give you praise

I give you praise, Lord
I give you praise
Because of your holiness
I give you praise
Though my sin is all I see,
You sent your Son to die for me
I give you praise, Lord
I give you praise

I give you praise, Lord
I give you praise
My hands lifted upward
to you in praise
I will raise my voice to sing
of glory and honor to our King
I give you praise, Lord
I give you praise

I praise you Lord, for you are worthy
I praise you Lord, for you are right
I praise you Lord for the victory
I have through your power and might

I thank you Lord for your mercy
I thank you Lord for your love
I thank you Lord for your grace
and your Son you sent down from above

O sovereign Lord make me humble
O sovereign Lord help me stand
O sovereign Lord make me willing
to place my life in your hands

There within the morning's dew,
the whisper of the dawn;
the furtive moments of the day,
from which my thoughts are drawn

The mystery itself takes form,
alights upon the mist;
the focus of my life is honed
unable to resist

The fruit of choices long ago
now ripened by God's hand;
the seeds of which are planted in
God's cultivated land

All the while the day is new,
still putting on it's face;
God's will for me comes into view:
the mystery takes place

He moves within my spirit
and asks me to obey;
and gives me strength to follow him
for yet another day

Holy, holy, holy is the Lamb;
Holy, holy is the "Great I Am"
Comforter, counsellor, mercy in His hand
Holy, holy, holy is the Lamb

Glory, glory, glory to the King
Glory, glory let all creation sing
Mighty God, Prince of Peace,
praise is what we bring
Glory, glory, glory to the King

Worthy, worthy, worthy is our God
Worthy, worthy hail and bring Him laud
Everlasting Father, spread His word abroad
Worthy, worthy, worthy is our God

Inspired by Jeremiah 17:7-8
Blessed is he who trusts the Lord,
with confidence in Him;
his life a tree grown by the stream,
its roots spread deep within
A tree that does not fear the heat
or worry of a drought;
its leaves remain forever green
and bears its fruit throughout

The rain falls on my consciousness
obscuring what I feel;
existence becomes waterlogged
and nothing appears real

A leak begins to formulate
in what were once my dreams;
they start to soften from within
and nothing's what it seems

A time for renovation comes,
a gutting of the past;
the tearing down of strongholds starts
and nothing's due to last

God's restoration work begins,
the healing process comes;
the Master Builder affects repairs
and nothing blocks the SON

You can never be certain of how life will be
Your purpose is not always easy to see
You may never find answers to questions you raise
But you'll always find God in the midst of praise

Though you aren't always privy to
God's sovereign plans,
and your efforts fall short of His
righteous commands
Yet He asks you to seek Him,
as He orders your days;
and you'll always find God
in the midst of praise

If you raise up your voice and worship His name,
and you lift holy hands with the chorus' refrain;
you'll find defeat leaves while victory stays
Oh, you'll always find God in the
midst of praise!

The morning rises sleepily
In soft and subtle hues
God's face upon the pastel sky
His glory shining through

The earth has opened up its eyes
For yet another day
Creation sings God's praises
While trees fold their limbs to pray

The wind and water start to stretch:
God's whisper in the breeze
The diamond tips upon the waves,
reflecting through the trees

Bird and fowl on the wing,
flowers in their beds;
dependent on the sovereign Lord
providing daily bread

Seasons, sunlight, moon and stars
all move in one accord
The provisions of our Lord stand firm
as promised in His Word

A farmer, so the Bible reads,
went out one day to sow his seed;
to gain a crop from all his toil
-Lord, help me be the good soil

Don't let the seed sown on the path,
and eaten in the aftermath,
the message of your Word to spoil
-Lord, help me be the good soil

And seed that fell upon the rock,
initial joy give way to shock;
and trouble cause me to recoil
-Lord, help me be the good soil

Let not the thorns along the way,
choke out what fruit I might display;
and worry be my constant foil
-Lord, help me be the good soil

Lord help me yield a crop that grows
a hundred, sixty, thirty fold;
a serving heart that's true and loyal
-Lord, help me be the good soil

My energy and time were spent
on whom my soul was paying rent;
and living where my loyalties lie,
I found the price was far too high

Only surrender would suffice,
a holy, living sacrifice;
conformed no longer to the world,
a mind transformed by God unfurled

And with God's mercy in full view,
I'd offer God the worship due;
enabling me to test and see
His good and perfect will for me

And then, with sober judgement sought,
not think more highly than I ought;
according to faith given free,
the measure of God's love for me

Where Eagles Fly

Their wingtips stretched beneath the sun
while holding it in place;
they soar above the mountain tops
determined in their pace

They ride the wind expectantly,
the owners of the sky;
suspended in the noble space
that's where the eagles fly

Surveying from a lofty perch,
insistent in their task;
they take no more than what is due,
than what they need to ask

As such they're known for freedom,
where strength and beauty lie;
unwavering upon the breeze
that's where the eagles fly

Sometimes in the midst of strain
you start to turn around;
and realize within the pain
the way to up is down

You recognize the same refrain
as you are "going through";
remember you've been there before,
that none of this is new

The old façade no longer works,
a coat of cheap veneer;
the finish must be stripped away
and faith replace the fear

A willingness to trust the Lord,
give all your cares to Him;
and let Him guide you through the trials,
let healing start within

When we sing Amazing Grace,
do we know what it entails?
A God who sacrificed Himself,
and our own efforts failed

When we sing Amazing Grace,
are we bolstered in our faith?
As Jesus leads us through our trials
to our pre-destined place

When we sing Amazing Grace,
are we thankful to our Lord?
His love transcending all our sin
while victory was scored

When we sing Amazing Grace,
can we look beyond our tears?
To stand behind God's mighty shield
and live beyond our fears

Are you there, Lord?
Are you listening to my cry?
Can't you see that I'm in pain?
Don't you hear me asking why?

Are you there, Lord?
Will you come and stop the tears?
Will you hold me in your arms
and alleviate my fears?

Do you care, Lord
that I waste away inside,
that each day is like the other,
with no time to stem the tide?

Take me there, Lord
to your place of peace and rest;
for in you I hope and trust,
as my faith's put to the test

Let me share, Lord
in your vision for the world;
and gain the strength to serve you,
as I feed upon your word

Someday I'll sing the victory song,
as day retreats, the shadows long;
and moonlight scampers to it's place
Someday I'll sing the victory song

Someday I'll lay my burdens down,
discarded on that hallowed ground;
and take instead God's offered grace
Someday I'll lay my burdens down

Someday I'll make it to the prize,
a lifetime's struggles to demise;
and finally climb the mountain face
Someday I'll make it to the prize

Someday I'll see Him face to face,
the Lord returning to his place;
and I shall know Him as He is
Someday I'll see Him face to face

In waters calm or tempest tossed,
the Lord controls the fury fare;
intent on searching for the lost,
from murky depths of deep despair

The Lord who keeps our lives afloat,
despite the stormy ocean waves;
though violent seas surround the boat,
those who trust in Him are saved

The ship that's tossed before the waves,
shall find it's ballast holding fast;
the keel aright, it's balance saved,
holds strong until the storm is past

And then the captain of our souls,
will safely lead us to the shore;
through time and worry, comfort tolls,
secure within His quiet moor

The transformation from within,
restored by His divine decree;
equipped to go back out again,
to rescue others trapped at sea

When the clouds obscure the sun
and the waves eclipse the sea;
and the wind berates the beachfront
as the morning shadows flee

While the day begins retreating
so the night can take its turn;
and the earth makes revolutions
which allow the moon to learn

Though the sky must change it's settings
so in keeping with the time;
yet the lightning flashes boldly
and the thunder plays it's chimes

So the Lord maintains the balance,
turning neither left nor right;
He presides o'er the proceedings
with His majesty in sight

His reflection in creation
as displayed for all to view;
and all nature in its beauty
ascribe God the glory due

Often life obscures our view,
our focus on the Lord askew
We haven't got the slightest clue
what we were put on earth to do

We count on what we like to do,
gifts and training we've been through;
which sometimes bears resemblance to
what we were put on earth to do

With trust in God we must pursue
God-given tasks that He foreknew;
specifically pertaining to
what we were put on earth to do

And driven by our love for you,
Lord, help us worship you anew;
and spur us on to see and do
what we were put on earth to do

CPSIA information can be obtained
at www.ICGtesting.com
Printed in the USA
LVHW021641120423
744200LV00009B/305